This book of Washington D.C. belongs to:

_____

Doodle your own self-portrait.

Book design: Charla Pettingill

Scanner Magician Extraordinaire: Melissa Fitzgerald

First Edition

ISBN: 978-1-938093-06-7

Printed in China

CPSIA Compliance Information: Batch #091512DP
For further information contact Duo Press, LLC at info@duopressbooks.com

duopress
www.duopressbooks.com

DOODLE
Washington D.C.

By Laura Krauss Melmed • Illustrations by Violet Lemay

duopress

Ready?

Go!

Welcome to Washington D.C.

Put a Washington scene inside this **snow globe.**

·Washington D.C.·

It's a nice day. **Draw the sun and a few clouds** over the Washington D.C. skyline.

It's a rainy day. Doodle the rain.

The sun came out! Doodle a rainbow.

Night has fallen. Doodle the moon and stars.

It's cherry blossom time!
Doodle lots of flowers on the trees.

Now **doodle some ducks** swimming in the
Tidal Basin.

Give the **White House** windows, columns, and chimneys.

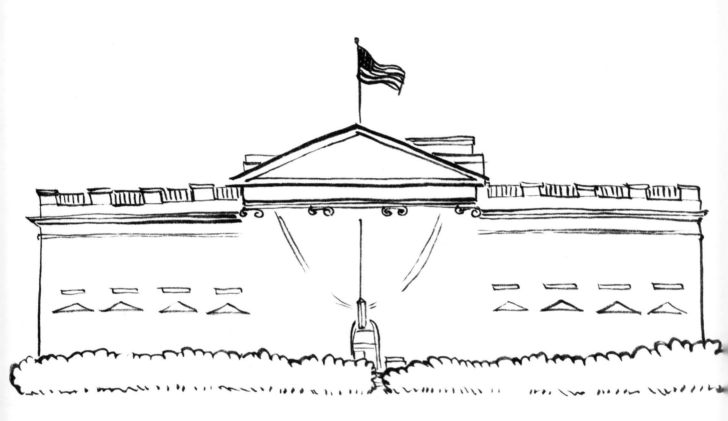

The president lives and works in the White House.

Give each child an **Easter egg** to roll.

The White House Easter Egg Roll takes place every year.

Decorate some **colorful flags** in front of these embassies.

Representatives from other countries live
and work at these embassies.

What's onstage at the **Kennedy Center?**

Who is in the **spotlight?**

Doodle some ways people might get to the city.
By car, train, plane, bus, taxi, or skateboard.

Doodle the **horses on the carousel** and some children riding the horses.

Finish this **dinosaur** at the Museum of Natural History.

These people are going to work.
They need faces!

Fill these baskets at the **farmers' market** with lots of healthy fruits and veggies.

Decorate this D.C. T-shirt.
Then, doodle some more cool T-shirts.

Color these tropical birds at the **National Zoo.**

Now **doodle your own** tropical birds!

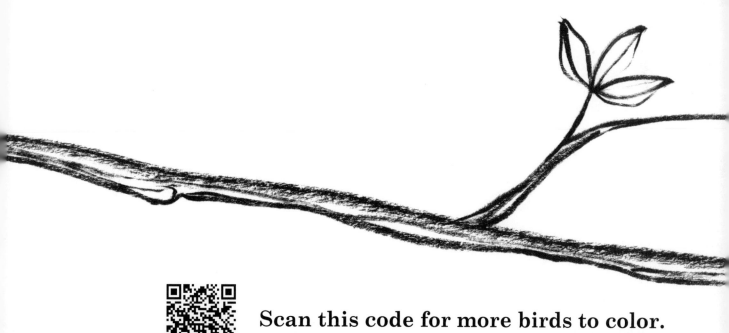

Scan this code for more birds to color.

Give these **zoo elephants** their trunks!

About 2,000 animals from 400 different species live at the National Zoo.

What time is it?
Doodle the hands on the clock at the Old Post Office.

The *Spirit of St. Louis* hangs at the Air and Space Museum.

Doodle its wings.

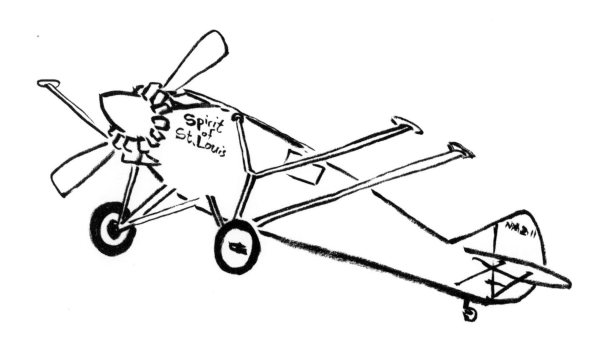

In this plane, Charles Lindbergh flew from New York to Paris in 1927, the first time anyone had ever flown across the Atlanic Ocean alone.

Now doodle a **crazy** plane!

This **Metrobus** needs a driver.

Take the **Doodle Challenge:**

This D.C. flag lost its stars.

Look at the sample, then doodle the stars with your eyes closed.

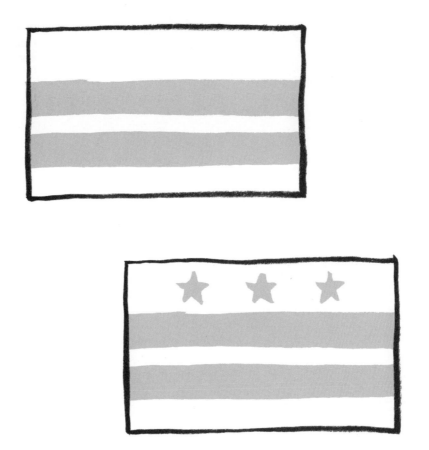

Four more Doodle Challenges to come!

What is your **favorite thing to do** in **summertime** in Washington D.C.?

What is your favorite thing to do in wintertime in Washington D.C.?

Doodle a **modern sculpture** for the sculpture park.

The National Gallery Sculpture Garden is filled with modern sculptures, including a giant eraser!

Doodle some visitors to the
Martin Luther King, Jr. memorial.

This messenger **needs** a bicycle.

Mama panda is hungry.

Doodle a big clump of bamboo for her to chomp on.

You can see pandas in action at the
National Zoo.

Doodle **your own** Metro map.
Make up some cool new stops.

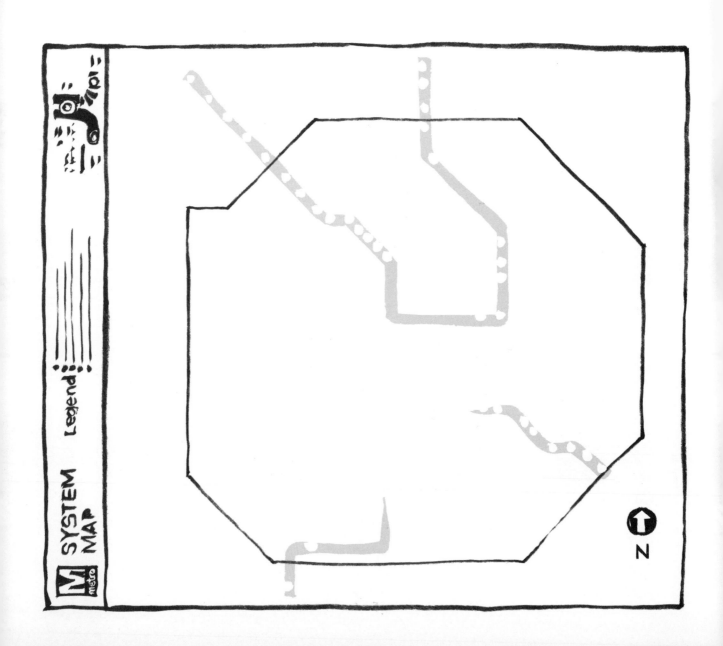

Doodle some passengers on this Metro train.

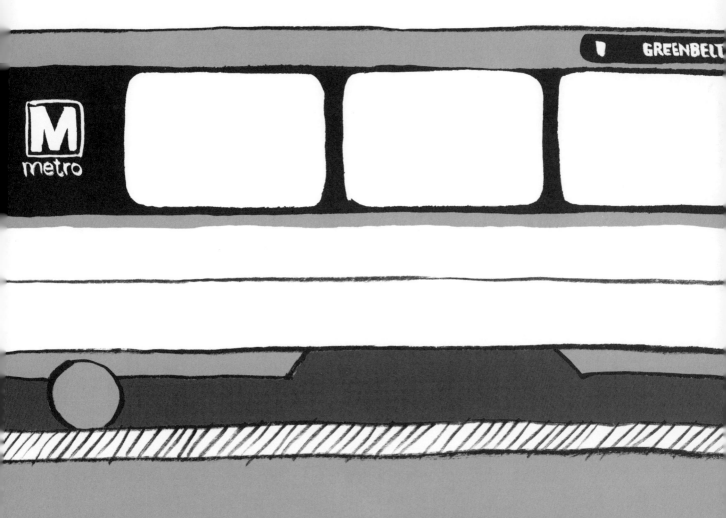

Fill in the columns on the **Lincoln Memorial.**

Fill in **President Lincoln's chair.**

The Lincoln Memorial honors President Abraham Lincoln.

Who is riding on these Segways?

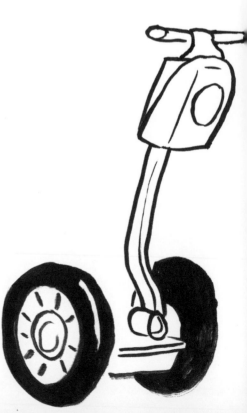

Doodle another dancer at the Latino Festival.

Draw the cover of your own book.

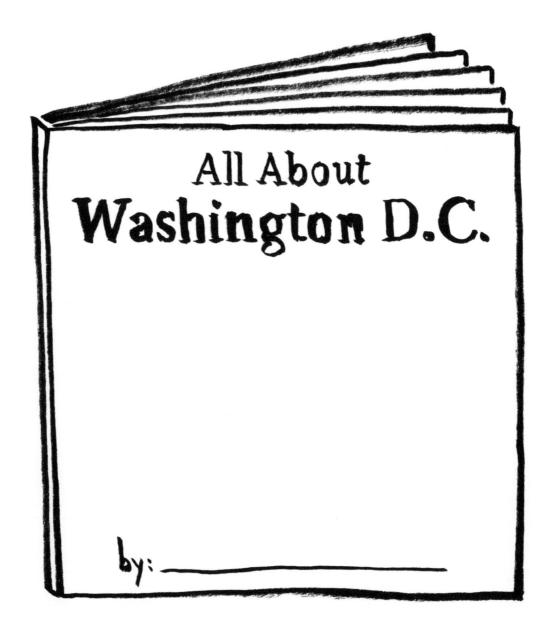

All About
Washington D.C.

by: _____

Take the **Doodle Challenge:**

This D.C. flag lost its stripes.

Look at the sample, then doodle the stripes with your eyes closed.

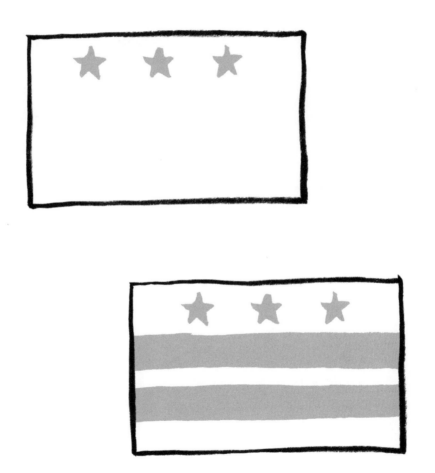

Three more Doodle Challenges to come!

Connect the **two sides** of the Key Bridge.

Put yourself in front of the camera and on-screen at the Newseum.

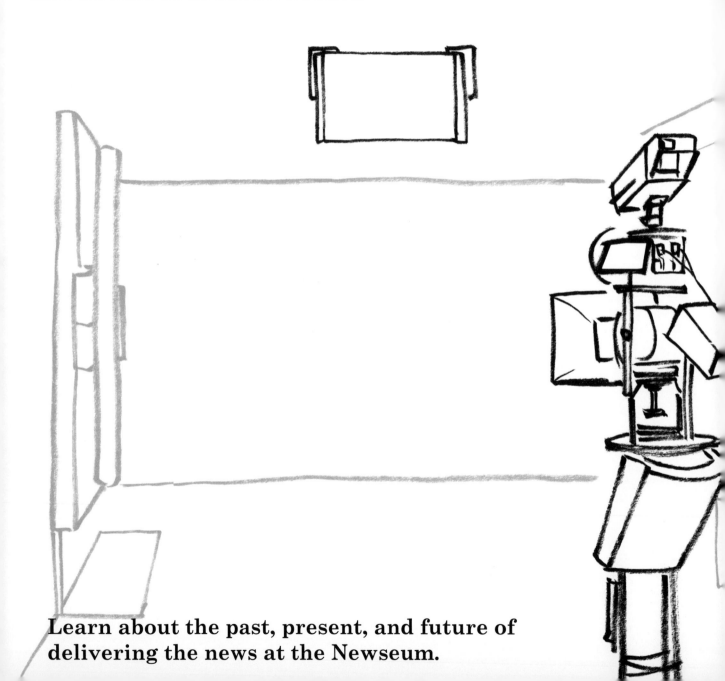

Learn about the past, present, and future of delivering the news at the Newseum.

Give this **Nationals** catcher a mitt.

Doodle **your favorite** Nats player hitting a home run.

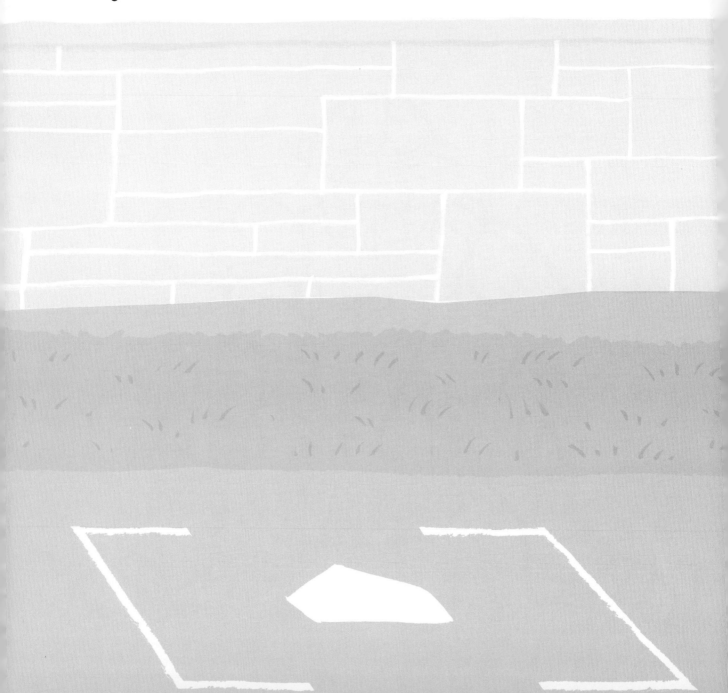

Doodle your favorite Redskins player making a touchdown.

Doodle your favorite Wizard scoring.

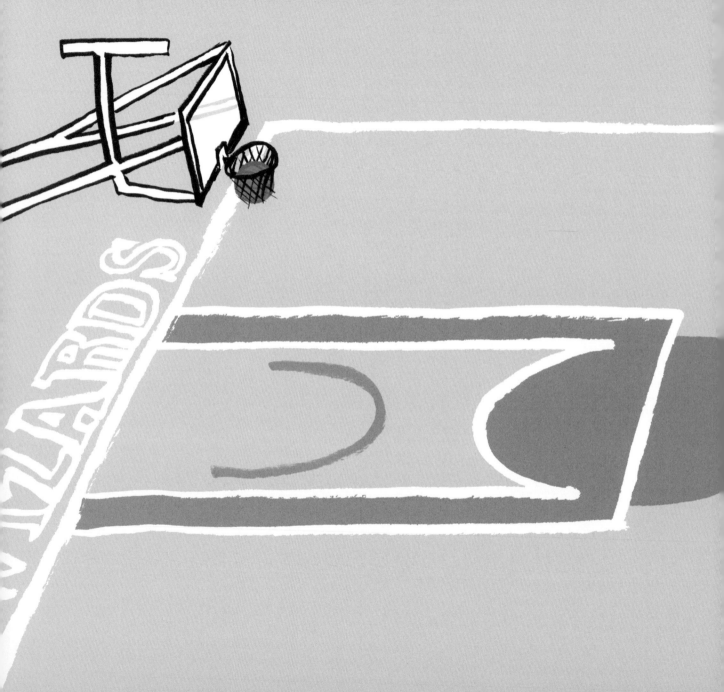

Great save by D.C. United! Doodle the goal and the ball.

Decorate these cupcakes. Use lots of colors.

It's a picnic in **Rock Creek Park.**
What's for lunch?

These kids are flying kites!
Doodle them!

The Blossom Kite Festival takes place on the Mall every spring.

Whose shadow is this?
Watch out!

You can be a spy at the Spy Museum.

Take the Doodle Challenge:

Doodle the missing star using one single line.

Two more Doodle Challenges to come!

It's July Fourth! Doodle some fabulous fireworks over the Washington Monument.

What is your favorite Washington restaurant meal?
Doodle it here.

Doodle some instruments for the
National Symphony Orchestra.

**The National Symphony Orchestra plays at
the Kennedy Center.**

This **paddleboat** needs some pedalers.

You can rent a paddleboat at the Tidal Basin.

Doodle some bicycle riders
on the **C&O Canal towpath.**

**The Chesapeake & Ohio Canal runs along
the Potomac River.**

This horse in **Rock Creek Park** needs a saddle.

The Rock Creek Park Horse Center offers lessons and trail rides through the park.

She made it! This runner is crossing the finish line. Doodle the banner.

The Marine Corps Marathon is held every fall for up to 30,000 competitors.

This fire truck needs its wheels and ladder.

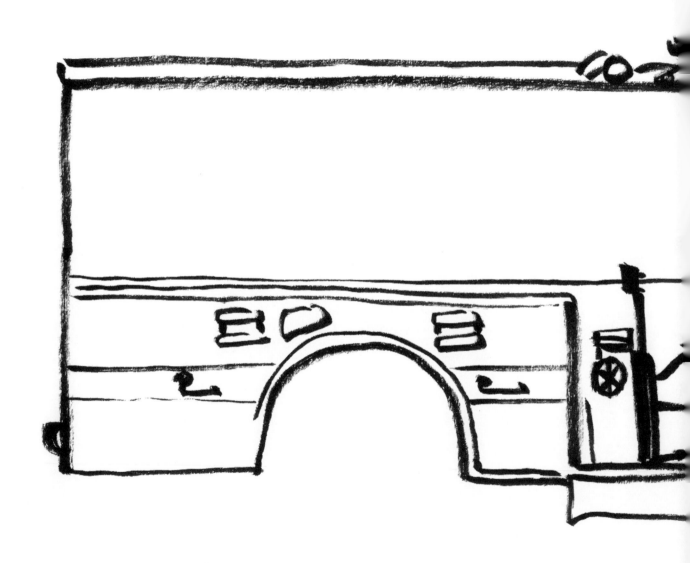

Doodle your own modern sculpture in front of the
Hirshhorn Museum.

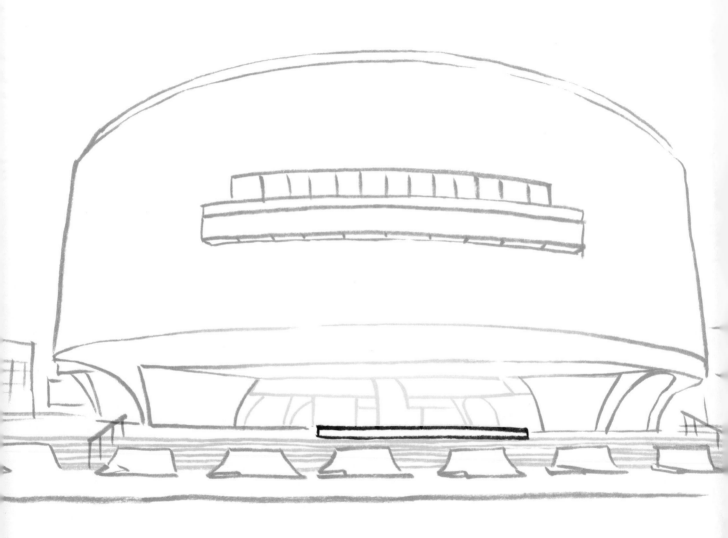

Draw some tropical plants at the **Botanic Garden.**

Doodle yourself next to Henry the elephant.

Henry is happy to welcome you to the
Smithsonian National Museum of Natural History.

Doodle **some joggers** on the Capital Crescent Trail.

Capital Crescent Trail
Department of Parks
Montgomery County

The Capital Crescent Trail runs from Georgetown to Silver Spring, Maryland.

Scan this code to get more joggers to color.

It's the **Chinese New Year parade.**
Doodle this dragon's head.

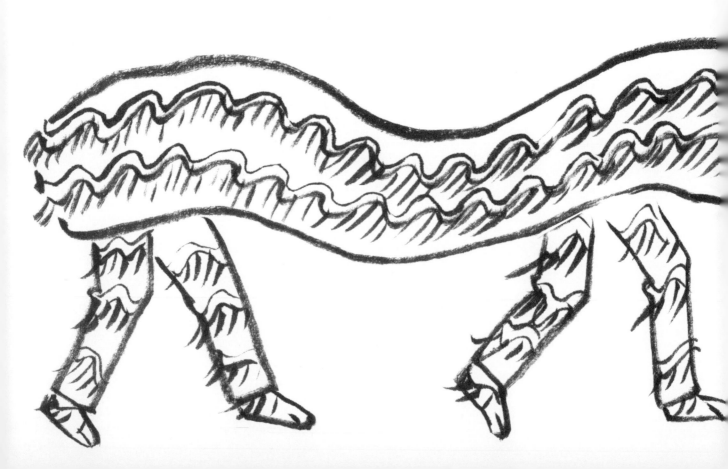

It's Halloween. Who is wearing these hats and masks?

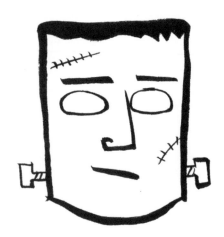

Now put **masks and hats** on these people.

Take the Doodle Challenge:

Are you right-handed? Doodle the flag with your left hand!
If you are left-handed use your right hand!

One more Doodle Challenge to come!

Doodle **tons of books** in your favorite store.

Scan this code to get some book covers to decorate.

Doodle the staircase on the **Old Stone House.**

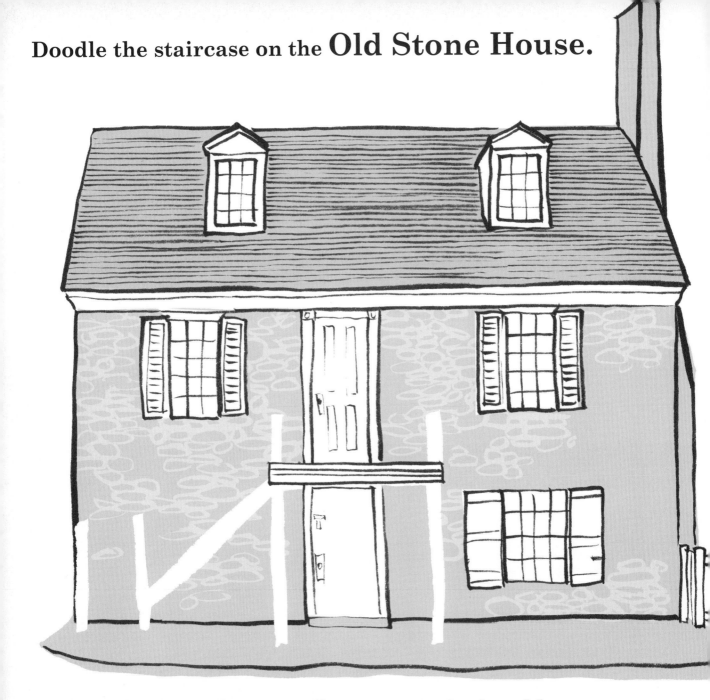

The Old Stone House in Georgetown is the oldest building in Washington D.C.

Please put lights on the **National Christmas Tree.**

Color these row houses in bright colors. Park some cars in front.

Doodle some portraits for these frames at the
National Gallery of Art.

This coyote mask is at the
National Museum of the American Indian.
Doodle some more masks!

Who is walking this dog?

This street musician **needs a violin and a bow.**

Doodle **someone diving** off the board
at the community pool.

Take the **Doodle Challenge:**

Doodle the flag using two hands and two pencils at the same time!

Washington D.C. is named after our first president.
Doodle George Washington's wig.

The **Jefferson Memorial** has lost its dome. Doodle it!

Doodle some animals in ZooLights!

ZooLights animals light up the National Zoo
during the winter holidays.

Fill your favorite toy store with awesome toys.

Doodle some boats in the
Holiday Boat Parade of Lights.

This boat parade on the Potomac River sails every December from Alexandria, Virginia.

This Metropolitan Police car needs its wheels.
Doodle them.

Scan this to get more cool vehicles to doodle!

Give these firefighters their helmets.

Doodle a horse for General Grant's statue.

Washington D.C. has more statues of men on horseback than any other city in the U.S.

Doodle some squirrels in the park.

Doodle the columns on the National Archives.

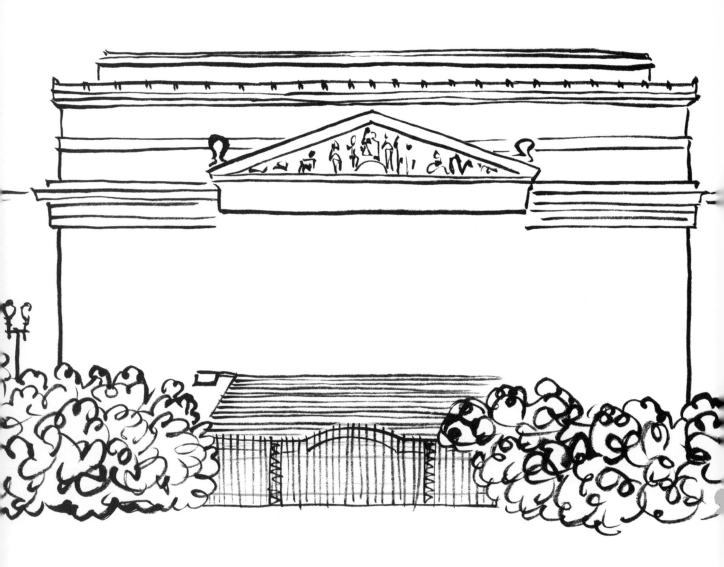

Visit the Archives to see the original
Declaration of Independence.

What's the next move?
Doodle this chess player's partner.

Dupont Circle is a meeting place for chess players.

It's nighttime. Doodle some constellations.

Finish the **Memorial Bridge.**

Doodle **lots** of books!

The Library of Congress is the largest library in the world!

Doodle the towers on the Smithsonian Castle.

It's the drum circle at **Meridian Hill Park!**
Doodle the drums.

This is the FBI building.
Doodle some spies **hiding around!**

Fill your **photo album** with memories of Washington D.C.

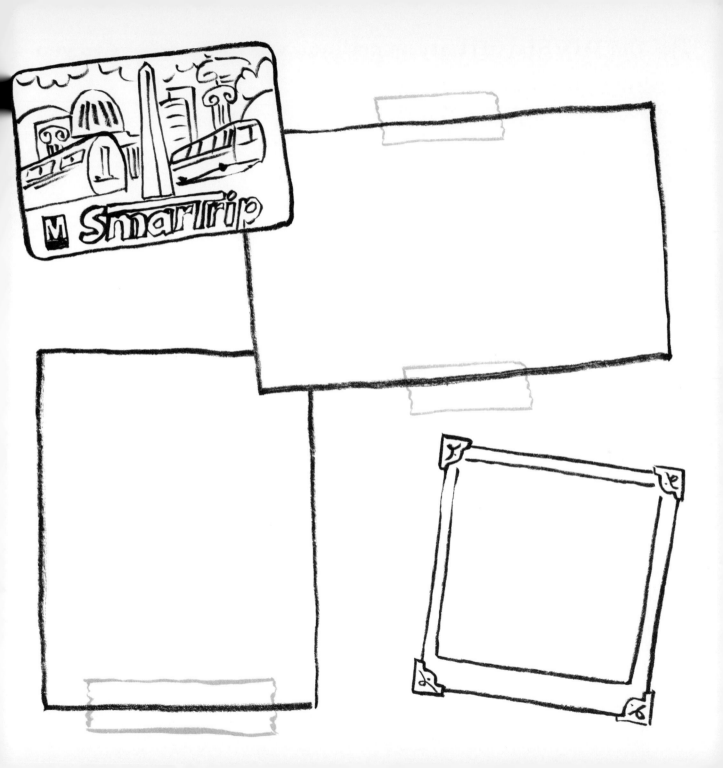

Put the president at the podium, waving good-bye to you!

Now, doodle **yourself** as the president!

Doodle yourself inside this space capsule!

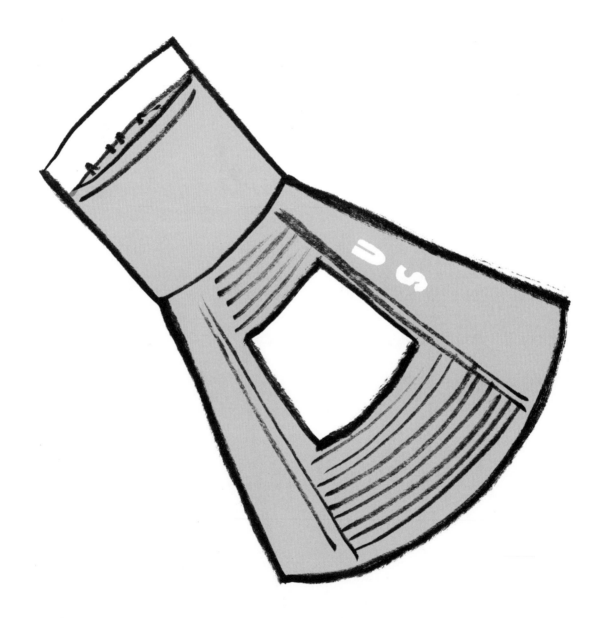

You can see many flying machines at
the Air and Space Museum.